Writing Garden

Student book

2

This book belongs to:

How to Use **Writing Garden**

Writing Prompt

A. Understand the Prompt

Students read and circle the important words. They learn how to understand the question properly and how to prepare for what they will write on their own.

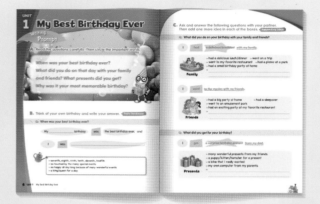

B. Topic Sentence

Students answer the given question for their own topic sentence. Expressions are provided to guide the students.

C. Supporting Ideas

Students ask and answer the questions with their partners. After that, they add one more idea in the blank. This speaking activity will help the students to practice developing relevant supporting ideas, and it will reinforce the acquisition of some of the many different expressions in English. This will also help the students to produce more ideas for their own writing. Expressions are provided to guide the students.

Writing Sprouts

A. Story

Students talk about the pictures and try to guess what the story is about. They learn the key vocabulary with the help of the pictures.

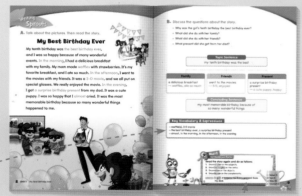

B. Questions with the Graphic Organizer

This comprehension activity will help the students to understand the story better. Students also learn how the ideas are developed and organized with the help of the graphic organizer.

Key Vocabulary & Expressions

Students learn the key vocabulary and expressions.

Hunt for Sentence Parts

Students learn sentence structure by identifying the subject and verb in a sentence.

C. Topic Sentence

Students choose the best topic sentence for the picture. Students learn what makes a proper topic sentence.

D. Details

Students read the story again and write correct details for the given supporting ideas. This will help the students learn how the supporting ideas and details are written to support the topic sentence.

Writing Process

Planning

Students brainstorm their ideas with the teacher and write them in the blanks. Students are encouraged to write any ideas that come to mind. The activities in *Writing Prompt* can help to guide the students.

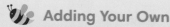

Adding Your Own

Depending on the level of the students, they can either use the examples in the box to answer the questions, or they can write their own answers to the questions. This activity helps the students practice writing a paragraph by incorporating a topic sentence, supporting ideas, and a concluding sentence.

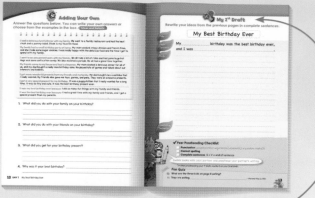

Gathering & Organizing

Students develop and organize their own ideas from the planning stage. The idea organizer will guide the students in writing their ideas in a more organized way.

My 1st Draft

Through the activity of rewriting the story, students can learn how a paragraph is developed, while at the same time reinforcing good writing skills. Students peer check their writing using the checklist at the bottom of the page. This will help the students to learn correct sentence structure.

Workbook

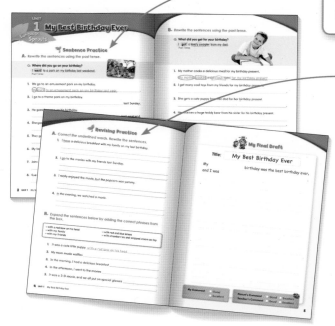

Sentence Practice

Students perform exercises in sentence-combining, subject-verb agreement, and various grammar constructs.

Revising Practice

Students find mistakes and correct them. Students also expand the sentences using the given words. This activity will help the students learn how to revise their writing and learn how to write longer sentences.

My Final Draft

Students make sure there are no mistakes in their final draft. Students can experience and understand the entire writing process by going through the exercises given, from the first step (Planning) to the last step (My Final Draft).

Contents

Example: Danny plants flowers.

My hero is my dad.

C (complement)

O (object)

V (verb)

S (subject)

●	S (subject)
■	V (verb)
★	O (object)
◗	C (complement)

Danny plants flowers.
S: Who plants flowers? Danny.
V: What does Danny do? He plants flowers.
O: What does Danny plant? He plants flowers.

My hero is my dad.
C: Who is your hero? My hero is my dad.

Writing Prompt

A. Read the questions carefully. Then circle the important words.

When was your best birthday ever?
What did you do on that day with your family
and friends? What presents did you get?
Why was it your most memorable birthday?

B. Think of your own birthday and write your answer. ◀ Topic Sentence

Q: When was your best birthday ever?

My _____ birthday   was   the best birthday ever,   and

I   was   _____ .

- seventh, eighth, ninth, tenth, eleventh, twelfth
- so touched by the many special events
- so happy all day long because of many wonderful events
- a king/queen for a day

C. Ask and answer the following questions with your partner. Then add one more idea in each of the boxes. Supporting Ideas

Q: What did you do on your birthday with your family and friends?

I   had   a delicious breakfast <u>with my family</u>.

Family

- had a delicious lunch/dinner
- went on a trip
- went to my favorite restaurant
- had a picnic at a park
- had a small birthday party at home
- _____

I   went   <u>to the movies with my friends</u>.

Friends

- had a big party at home
- had a sleepover
- went to an amusement park
- had an exciting party at my favorite restaurant
- _____

Q: What did you get for your birthday?

I   got   a surprise birthday present <u>from my dad</u>.

Presents

- many wonderful presents from my friends
- a puppy/kitten/hamster for a present
- a bike that I really wanted
- my own computer from my parents
- _____

7

A. Talk about the pictures. Then read the story.

My Best Birthday Ever

My tenth birthday was the best birthday ever, and I was so happy because of many wonderful events. In the morning, I had a delicious breakfast with my family. My mom made waffles with strawberries. It's my favorite breakfast, and I ate so much. In the afternoon, I went to the movies with my friends. It was a 3-D movie, and we all put on special glasses. We really enjoyed the movie. In the evening, I got a surprise birthday present from my dad. It was a cute puppy. I was so happy that I almost cried. It was the most memorable birthday because so many wonderful things happened to me.

B. Discuss the questions about the story.

- Why was the girl's tenth birthday the best birthday ever?
- What did she do with her family?
- What did she do with her friends?
- What present did she get from her dad?

Topic Sentence
my tenth birthday was the best

Family
a delicious breakfast
→ waffles, ate so much

Friends
went to the movies
→ 3-D, enjoyed

Present
a surprise birthday present
→ a cute puppy, happy

Concluding Sentence
my most memorable birthday because of so many wonderful things

Key Vocabulary & Expressions

- waffle(s), 3-D movie
- the best birthday ever, a surprise birthday present
- almost, in the morning, in the afternoon, in the evening

Hunt for Sentence Parts

Read the story again and do as follows:
1. Draw circles on the subjects.
2. Draw rectangles on the verbs.
3. Draw stars on the objects.
4. Draw leaves on the complements.

Example I got a surprise birthday present from my dad.

Subject Ⓢ
Verb Ⓥ
Object Ⓞ
Complement Ⓒ

C. Choose the best topic sentence for the picture.

A Kittens are so cute.

B My ninth birthday was my best birthday ever because my sister gave me a kitten.

C My eleventh birthday was the best birthday ever because I did many special things.

D This is my best birthday party.

D. Read the *Writing Sprouts* story again and write the details.

1. I had a delicious breakfast with my family.

   My mom made waffles with strawberries _____.

   It's my favorite breakfast, and I ate so much _____.

2. I went to the movies with my friends.

   It was _____.

   We _____.

3. I got a surprise birthday present from my dad.

   It was _____.

   I _____.

Writing Process

Planning

Brainstorm and write your ideas. Any idea is all right. You can use the words and phrases on the *Writing Prompt* (pp. 6–7).

_____   _____

_____   _____

_____   _____

_____

Topic
My Best Birthday Ever

Gathering & Organizing

Gather and organize your ideas in the correct boxes.

Topic: **My Best Birthday Ever**

Topic Sentence

My _____ birthday was the best birthday ever,
and I was _____.

Family	Friends	Present
I _____ _____ . _____ _____ .	I _____ _____ . _____ _____ .	I got _____ _____ . _____ _____ .

Concluding Sentence

It was the most memorable birthday because _____ .

Adding Your Own

Answer the questions below. You can write your own answers or choose from the examples in the box. Ideas and Details

I had a delicious lunch/dinner with my family. We went to a family restaurant and had the best steak and a yummy salad. Steak is my favorite food.

My family had a small birthday party at home. My mom cooked crispy chicken and French fries, and she made some sugar cookies. I was really happy with the delicious food and the time I got to spend with my family.

I went to an amusement park with my friends. We all rode a lot of rides and had some huge hot dogs and some soft cotton candy. We also watched a parade. We all had a great time together.

My friends came to my house and had a sleepover. My mom cooked a delicious dinner for all of us, and my dad bought a really nice birthday cake. We played lots of games and talked about our interests and hobbies.

I got many wonderful presents from my friends and my family. My dad bought me a cool bike that I really wanted. My friends also gave me toys, games, and pens. They were all awesome presents.

I got a very special present for my birthday. It was a puppy/kitten that I really wanted for a long time. It was so tiny and cute. It was the best birthday present ever.

It was my best birthday ever because I did so many fun things with my family and friends.

It was the best birthday ever because I had a great time with my family and friends, and I got a special present from my parents.

1. What did you do with your family on your birthday?

   _____

   _____

   _____

2. What did you do with your friends on your birthday?

   _____

   _____

   _____

3. What did you get for your birthday present?

   _____

   _____

   _____

4. Why was it your best birthday? _____

   _____

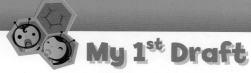

My 1ˢᵗ Draft

Rewrite your ideas from the previous pages in complete sentences.

Title

My Best Birthday Ever

Topic Sentence

My _____ birthday was the best birthday ever, and I was _____.

Body

_____

_____

_____

_____

_____

_____

_____

_____

_____

_____

_____

Concluding Sentence

_____

_____

✔ **Peer Proofreading Checklist:**

☐ **Punctuation** ✔capitalization ✔commas(,) ✔periods(.) ✔question marks(?)

☐ **Correct spelling**

☐ **Complete sentences** S + V + end of sentence

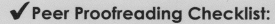
Switch books with your partner and proofread your partner's writing.

↱ After proofreading your 1ˢᵗ draft, rewrite it on your final draft.

Fun Quiz

Q: What are the three kids on page 8 eating?

A: They are eating _____. <Answer Key p. 80>

Writing Prompt

A. Read the questions carefully. Then circle the important words.

What is your favorite food? Why do you like it? Give three reasons with details.

Topic Sentence

B. Think of your own favorite food and write your answer.

Q: What is your favorite food, and where is the food from?

My favorite food   is _____, and

it   is _____.

- pasta, spaghetti, fried chicken, roasted chicken
- a very famous Italian food   • an American food

C. Ask and answer the following questions with your partner. Then add one more idea in each of the boxes. ◀ **Supporting Ideas**

Q: What is so special about your favorite food?

I | can put | different toppings | on it.

Ingredients
- I can put different kinds of sauces on it.
- I can choose from many types of pasta.
- I can put different herbs and spices on it.
- I can enjoy various parts of the chicken.
- _____

Q: Why is your favorite food good for you?

It | is | good because **it makes my body stronger**.

Health Facts
- it makes me happy when I eat it   • it is healthy for me
- it is nutritious   • it has a lot of nutrients
- it has a lot of protein   • it makes me strong and healthy
- it gives me lots of energy
- _____

Q: How does your favorite food taste?

It | is | delicious.

Taste
- tasty   • spicy   • creamy   • crispy   • crunchy
- juicy   • sweet   • salty   • bitter   • sour
- buttery   • cheesy   • fruity
- _____

A. Talk about the pictures. Then read the story.

My Favorite Food

My favorite food is pizza, and it is a very famous Italian food. First, I love pizza because I can put different toppings on it. Some popular toppings are pepperoni, mushrooms, onions, and cheese. I can make many kinds of pizza with the toppings. Second, I love pizza because it is good for my body. Vegetables, meat, and cheese on the pizza have a lot of nutrients. Pizza makes me strong and healthy. Lastly, I love pizza because it is so delicious. The tomato sauce and the stringy cheese on the crust are just fantastic. I can eat pizza every day. I think pizza is the best food in the world.

B. Discuss the questions about the story.

- Where is pizza from?
- What is the first reason the boy loves pizza?
- What are some popular toppings?
- What is the second reason the boy loves pizza?
- How is the pizza good for his body?
- What is the last reason the boy loves pizza?

Topic Sentence
my favorite food is pizza, Italian food

Ingredients
different toppings
→ pepperoni, mushrooms, onions, and cheese
→ can make many kinds of pizza

Health Facts
good for my body
→ a lot of nutrients
→ makes me strong and healthy

Taste
so delicious
→ tomato sauce and stringy cheese
→ can eat it every day

Concluding Sentence
the best food in the world

Key Vocabulary & Expressions

- topping(s), pepperoni, mushroom(s), vegetable(s), meat, nutrient(s), sauce, crust
- Italian, popular, healthy, stringy, fantastic

Hunt for Sentence Parts

Read the story again and do as follows:
1. Draw circles on the subjects.
2. Draw rectangles on the verbs.
3. Draw stars on the objects.
4. Draw leaves on the complements.

Example My favorite food is pizza.

Subject Ⓢ
Verb Ⓥ
Object Ⓞ
Complement Ⓒ

C. Choose the best topic sentence for the picture.

A Pizza is the best food because of the different toppings, nutrients, and taste.

B Fried chicken is a noodle dish.

C Pizza is my favorite topping.

D Fried chicken is my favorite food in the world.

D. Read the *Writing Sprouts* story again and write the details.

1. I love pizza because I can put different toppings on it.

   Some popular toppings are pepperoni, mushrooms, onions, and cheese .

   I can make many kinds of pizza with the toppings .

2. I love pizza because it is good for my body.

   Vegetables, meat, and cheese on the pizza _____.

   Pizza _____.

3. I love pizza because it is so delicious.

   The tomato sauce and the stringy cheese on the crust _____.

   I _____.

Writing Process

Planning

Brainstorm and write your ideas. Any idea is all right. You can use the words and phrases on the *Writing Prompt* (pp. 14–15).

Topic
My Favorite Food

_____

Gathering & Organizing

Gather and organize your ideas in the correct boxes.

Topic: My Favorite Food

Topic Sentence

My favorite food is _____, and it is _____
_____.

Ingredients	Health Facts	Taste
It is _____ _____ _____.	It is _____ _____ _____.	It is _____ _____ _____.

Concluding Sentence

I think _____ is the best food in the world.

Adding Your Own

Answer the questions below. You can write your own answers or choose from the examples in the box. Ideas and Details

I like pasta because I can put different kinds of sauces on it. Some popular sauces are tomato sauce, cream sauce, and olive oil sauce. I can make many kinds of pasta with the sauces.

I like fried chicken because I can put different seasonings and spices on it. Some popular seasonings and spices are salt, pepper, garlic powder, and parsley. I can enjoy the fried chicken with many types of dipping sauce.

I like pasta because it is healthy for me. The pasta and the sauce have a lot of nutrients. Pasta makes me strong and healthy.

I like fried chicken because it is nutritious. Chicken has a lot of protein. Fried chicken gives me lots of energy.

I like pasta because it is so tasty. Many kinds of pasta and sauces are just fantastic. I can eat pasta every day.

I like fried chicken because it is so crispy and crunchy. Juicy chicken with tasty seasonings and spices is just wonderful. I can eat fried chicken for breakfast, lunch, and dinner.

I think pasta is the best food in the world.

I think fried chicken is the best food in the world.

1. What is so special about your favorite food?

   _____

   _____

2. Why is your favorite food good for you?

   _____

   _____

3. How does your favorite food taste?

   _____

   _____

4. What do you think about your favorite food?

   _____

   _____

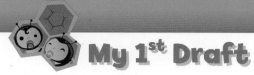 **My 1ˢᵗ Draft**

Rewrite your ideas from the previous pages in complete sentences.

Title

My Favorite Food

Topic
Sentence

My favorite food is _____, and it is

Body

_____.

_____

_____

_____

_____

_____

_____

_____

_____

_____

Concluding
Sentence

_____

_____

_____

✔ **Peer Proofreading Checklist:**

☐ **Punctuation** ✔capitalization ✔commas(,) ✔periods(.) ✔question marks(?)

☐ **Correct spelling**

☐ **Complete sentences** S + V + end of sentence

Switch books with your partner and proofread your partner's writing.

➜ After proofreading your 1ˢᵗ draft, rewrite it on your final draft.

Fun Quiz

Q: What kind of pizza is the boy on page 16 eating?

A: He is eating _____. <Answer Key p. 80>

3 Aunt Lucy, My Hero

Writing Prompt

A. Read the questions carefully. Then circle the important words.

Who is your hero?

Why is the person your hero? What did the person do for you that was so special?

Give three reasons with details.

Topic Sentence

B. Think of your own personal hero and write your answer.

Q: Who is your hero, and what is she/he like?

My hero   is   my _____, and

he / she   is   _____.

- mother, father, grandmother, grandfather, uncle, aunt, teacher, friend
- a good role model for me
- a great mentor
- the most wonderful person in the world

C. Ask and answer the following questions with your partner. Then add one more idea in each of the boxes. Supporting Ideas

Q: What sports or activities did your hero teach you?

He / She | taught | me how to <u>ride a bicycle</u>.

Sports/ Activities

- play baseball
- play soccer
- play basketball
- play tennis
- play chess
- inline skate
- skateboard
- swim
- do taekwondo
- ride a horse
- do cartwheels
- run very fast
- _____

Q: How did your hero help you learn things?

He / She | showed | me how important it is to <u>read books</u>.

Study

- do my best in school
- concentrate in class
- read newspapers
- do well in my studies
- read many books
- have curiosity
- _____

Q: How did your hero help you in your personal life?

He / She | helped | me to <u>make friends</u>.

Personal Life

- be brave and strong
- respect myself
- have many friends
- have patience
- have confidence in myself
- be kind and polite
- be a good listener
- _____

A. Talk about the pictures. Then read the story.

Aunt Lucy, My Hero

Dear Aunt Lucy,

You are my hero, and you are a great mentor. I will never forget all the things you taught me. First, you taught me how to ride a bicycle. At the park, you ran behind me to help me balance. I fell so many times, but you were a kind teacher. Next, you showed me how important it is to read books. You took me to the library every weekend. You encouraged me to read many kinds of books. Lastly, you helped me to make friends. I was shy and didn't have any friends, but you taught me to be brave. Now I have many friends. You will always have a special place in my heart. Thank you for being my hero, Aunt Lucy.

Love,
Andrew

B. Discuss the questions about the story.

- Who is Andrew's hero?
- Why is she Andrew's hero?
- What did Aunt Lucy do for him first?
- What did Aunt Lucy do for him second?
- What did Aunt Lucy do for him last?

Topic Sentence

Aunt Lucy, you are my hero and a great mentor.

Sports/Activities	**Study**	**Personal Life**
how to ride a bicycle → help me balance → a kind teacher	how important it is to read books → took me to the library → read many kinds of books	how to make friends → taught me to be brave → have many friends

Concluding Sentence

Thank you for being my hero.

Key Vocabulary & Expressions

- hero, mentor, library, weekend
- forget/forgot, teach/taught, balance/balanced, encourage/encouraged
- important, shy, brave

Hunt
for Sentence Parts

Read the story again and do as follows:
1. Draw circles on the subjects.
2. Draw rectangles on the verbs.
3. Draw stars on the objects.
4. Draw leaves on the complements.

Example You taught me how to ride a bicycle.

Subject Ⓢ
Verb Ⓥ
Object Ⓞ
Complement Ⓒ

C. Choose the best topic sentence for the picture.

A My father always watches TV at home.

B My grandmother is my hero, and she taught me so many things.

C My father is the hero of my life.

D My grandmother is sitting in the garden.

D. Read the *Writing Sprouts* story again and write the details.

1. First, you taught me how to ride a bicycle.

At the park, you ran behind me to help me balance   .

I fell so many times, but you were a kind teacher   .

2. Next, you showed me how important it is to read books.

You _____.

You _____.

3. Lastly, you helped me to make friends.

I was shy and didn't have any friends, but you _____

_____.

Now I _____.

 **Planning**

Brainstorm and write your ideas. Any idea is all right. You can use the words and phrases on the *Writing Prompt* (pp. 22–23).

_____   _____

_____   _____

_____   _____

_____   _____

Topic
My Hero

Gathering & Organizing

Gather and organize your ideas in the correct boxes.

Topic: _____ , **My Hero**

Topic Sentence

Dear _____ ,

You are my hero, and you are _____ .

Sports/Activities	Study	Personal Life
You taught me how to ___ _____ _____ _____ _____ .	You showed me how important it is to _____ _____ _____ _____ .	You helped me to _____ _____ _____ _____ _____ .

Concluding Sentence

Thank you for _____ .

Adding Your Own

Answer the questions below. You can write your own answers or choose from the examples in the box. < Ideas and Details

You taught me how to play baseball/soccer/basketball/tennis/chess/a board game. You carefully explained the rules of the game to me. I learned many useful skills from you.

You taught me how to inline skate/skateboard/swim/do taekwondo/ride a horse/do cartwheels/run very fast. You showed me how to keep my balance and move my arms and legs. You also explained some safety tips so that I wouldn't get hurt.

You showed me how important it is to study hard. You told me to study hard so that I could be anything I want to be. You encouraged me to set high goals for myself and never give up.

You showed me how important it is to read many books. You told me to read many books so that I could learn many things and be smart. You encouraged me to aim high and do my best.

You helped me to be brave and strong. I was scared of many things and was not very strong. You taught me to stand up for myself and to have courage.

You helped me to be kind and polite. You showed me what good manners are. You also taught me how to be understanding and how to share.

You will always have a special place in my heart. Thank you for being my hero.

You will always have a special place in my heart. Thank you for always being there for me.

1. What sports or activities did your hero teach you?

   _____

   _____

2. How did your hero help you study?

   _____

   _____

3. How did your hero help you in your personal life?

   _____

   _____

4. What do you want to say to your hero?

   _____

   _____

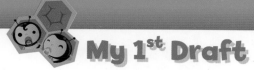

My 1st Draft

Rewrite your ideas from the previous pages in complete sentences.

_____, My Hero

Title

Topic Sentence

Dear _____,

You are my hero, and you are _____

_____ .

Body

_____

_____

_____

_____

_____

_____

_____

_____

_____

_____

Concluding Sentence

_____

_____

✔ **Peer Proofreading Checklist:**

☐ **Punctuation** ✔capitalization ✔commas(,) ✔periods(.) ✔question marks(?)

☐ **Correct spelling**

☐ **Complete sentences** S + V + end of sentence

Switch books with your partner and proofread your partner's writing.

↳ After proofreading your 1st draft, rewrite it on your final draft.

Fun Quiz

Q: What color is Andrew's bicycle on page 24?

A: It is _____ . <Answer Key p. 80>

UNIT 4 My Favorite Room

A. Read the questions carefully. Then circle the important words.

Which place in your home do you like the best?

What three things are special about this place?

Give reasons with details.

Topic Sentence

B. Think of your favorite place in your house and write your answer.

Q: Which place in your home do you like the best? What is it like?

_____ is the best place in my home because

it is very _____.

- My bedroom, My room, Our living room, Our family room
- cozy, comfortable, relaxing, charming, lovely, big, spacious, peaceful, quiet, private, large, dark, warm, bright

C. Ask and answer the following questions with your partner. Then add one more idea in each of the boxes. <Supporting Ideas

Q: What special furniture does your favorite place have?

It   has   a small bed   by the wall.

Furniture

- a soft bed near the window
- a big armchair next to the bed
- a large rocking chair by the bed
- a big sofa for my family to sit on
- a couch large enough for my family
- _____

Q: What special electronic device does it have?

It   has   a computer.

Electronics

- a computer on the desk
- a television with a big screen
- a home video-game console
- a lamp beside the bed
- a stereo with speakers
- _____

Q: What favorite thing of yours does it have?

It   has   a huge teddy bear.

Personal Favorite

- my favorite toys
- a lot of comic books
- a pretty ceiling light
- a coffee table in front of the sofa
- a family photo on the wall
- many interesting books
- a nice picture on the wall
- a grandfather clock by the wall
- _____

A. Talk about the pictures. Then read the story.

My Favorite Room

My bedroom is the best place in my home because it is really cozy. There are three things that make it so nice. First, my room has a small bed by the wall. The bed is just the right size, and it has a warm blanket on top. I love to be in my soft bed on a rainy day. Next, my room has a computer. It is on my desk, and it is very useful. I use my computer to do my homework. The last special thing is my huge teddy bear. It is brown and has a bow around its neck. I hug my teddy bear when I am sad. My cozy bedroom is a very special place to me in my home.

B. Discuss the questions about the story.

- Which place in the girl's home does she like the best?
- What is the place like?
- What is the first thing that she likes about the place?
- What is the second thing that she likes about the place?
- What is the last thing that she likes about the place?

Topic Sentence

my bedroom is the best place, cozy

Furniture

a small bed by the wall
→ right size, a warm blanket on top
→ love to be in my soft bed on a rainy day

Electronics

a computer
→ on my desk, very useful
→ do my homework

Personal Favorite

a huge teddy bear
→ brown and has a bow around its neck
→ hug my teddy bear when I am sad

Concluding Sentence

a very special place to me

Key Vocabulary & Expressions

- wall(s), blanket(s), homework, teddy bear(s), bow(s)
- cozy, rainy, useful, huge

Hunt for Sentence Parts

Read the story again and do as follows:
1. Draw circles on the subjects.
2. Draw rectangles on the verbs.
3. Draw stars on the objects.
4. Draw leaves on the complements.

Example My bedroom is the best place in my home.

Subject Ⓢ
Verb Ⓥ
Object Ⓞ
Complement Ⓒ

C. Choose the best topic sentence for the picture.

A My house has a huge kitchen.

B Of all the places in my house, I like the living room the best.

C My hobby is drawing pictures.

D My bedroom is my favorite place in my house.

D. Read the *Writing Sprouts* story again and write the details.

1. My room has a small bed by the wall.

   The bed is just the right size, and it has a warm blanket on top .

   I love to be in my soft bed on a rainy day .

2. My room has a computer.

   It is _____ .

   I _____ .

3. My room has a huge teddy bear.

   It is _____ .

   I _____ .

Writing Process

 **Planning**

Brainstorm and write your ideas. Any idea is all right. You can use the words and phrases on the *Writing Prompt* (pp. 30–31).

Topic
My Favorite Room

Gathering & Organizing

Gather and organize your ideas in the correct boxes.

Topic: My Favorite Room

Topic Sentence
_____ is the best place in my home because it is _____ _____. There are three things that make it so nice.

Furniture	Electronics	Personal Favorite
It has _____	It has _____	It has _____
_____.	_____.	_____.

Concluding Sentence
_____ is a very special place to me in my home.

Adding Your Own

Answer the questions below. You can write your own answers or choose from the examples in the box. ‹ **Ideas and Details**

My bedroom has a soft bed near the window. It is nice and comfortable. I like to relax in it when I am tired.

Our living room has a big sofa for my family to sit on. It is very nice and soft. I like to sit on it and relax.

My bedroom has a computer on the desk. It is awesome and very useful. I like to use it when I study or do my homework in my room.

Our living room has a television with a big screen. It is huge and very entertaining. I enjoy watching it when I am relaxing on the sofa.

My bedroom has my favorite toys. They are very fun and exciting. They keep me busy when I am bored.

Our living room has a nice picture on the wall. It is old and very valuable. The living room looks so beautiful with it.

My comfortable bedroom is a very special place to me in my home.

Our peaceful living room is a very special place to me in my home.

1. What special furniture is in your favorite place?

   _____

   _____

2. What special electronic device is in your favorite place?

   _____

   _____

3. What thing in your room is your personal favorite?

   _____

   _____

4. How do you feel about your favorite place in your home?

   _____

   _____

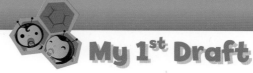

My 1st Draft

Rewrite your ideas from the previous pages in complete sentences.

Title

My Favorite Room

Topic Sentence

_____ is the best place in my home because

it is _____ . There are three things that

make it so nice.

Body

_____

_____

_____

_____

_____

_____

_____

_____

_____

Concluding Sentence

_____

_____

✔ **Peer Proofreading Checklist:**

☐ **Punctuation** ✔capitalization ✔commas(,) ✔periods(.) ✔question marks(?)

☐ **Correct spelling**

☐ **Complete sentences** S + V + end of sentence

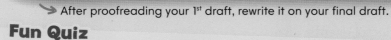

Switch books with your partner and proofread your partner's writing.

➔ After proofreading your 1st draft, rewrite it on your final draft.

Fun Quiz

Q: What color is the girl's blanket on page 32?

A: It is _____ . <Answer Key p. 80>

Review Units 1 & 2

A. Write the past tense.

1. am _____
2. make _____
3. go _____
4. enjoy _____
5. love _____

6. have _____
7. eat _____
8. put on _____
9. happen _____
10. is _____

B. Complete the topic and concluding sentences using the phrases from the box below.

1. My tenth birthday was the best birthday ever, and I was so _____

_____.

2. My favorite food is pizza, and _____

_____.

3. It was the most memorable birthday _____

_____.

4. I can eat pizza every day. I _____

_____.

- think pizza is the best food in the world
- because so many wonderful things happened to me
- it is a very famous Italian food
- happy because of many wonderful events

C. Write the proper supporting ideas from the box below.

1. _____

My mom made waffles with strawberries. It's my favorite breakfast, and I ate so much.

2. _____

It was a cute puppy. I was so happy that I almost cried.

3. _____

It was a 3-D movie, and we all put on special glasses. We really enjoyed the movie.

4. _____

The tomato sauce and the stringy cheese on the crust are just fantastic.

5. _____

Some popular toppings are pepperoni, mushrooms, onions, and cheese. I can make all kinds of pizza with the toppings.

6. _____

The vegetables, meat, and cheese on the pizza have a lot of nutrients. Pizza makes me strong and healthy.

- Lastly, I love pizza because it is so delicious.
- I went to the movies with my friends.
- First, I love pizza because I can put different toppings on it.
- I got a surprise birthday present from my dad.
- I had a delicious breakfast with my family.
- Second, I love pizza because it is good for my body.

 Activity cards are available at the back of the book.

A. Write the past tense.

1. are _____

2. forget _____

3. run _____

4. show _____

5. encourage _____

6. hug _____

7. teach _____

8. fall _____

9. take _____

10. help _____

B. Complete the topic and concluding sentences using the phrases from the box below.

1. You will always _____

_____.

2. My bedroom is the _____

_____.

3. My cozy bedroom is a _____

_____.

4. You are my hero, and you are a great mentor. I will _____

_____.

- never forget all the things you taught me
- best place in my home because it is really cozy
- have a special place in my heart
- very special place to me in my home

C. Write the proper supporting ideas from the box below.

1. _____

The bed is just the right size, and it has a warm blanket on top. I love to be in my soft bed on a rainy day.

2. _____

You took me to the library every weekend. You encouraged me to read many kinds of books.

3. _____

It is brown and has a bow around its neck. I hug my teddy bear when I am sad.

4. _____

I was shy and didn't have any friends, but you taught me to be brave. Now I have many friends.

5. _____

At the park, you ran behind me to help me balance. I fell so many times, but you were a kind teacher.

6. _____

It is on my desk, and it is very useful. I use my computer to do my homework.

- First, you taught me how to ride a bicycle.
- Lastly, you helped me to make friends.
- The last special thing is my huge teddy bear.
- Next, you showed me how important it is to read books.
- First, my room has a small bed by the wall.
- Next, my room has a computer.

 Activity cards are available at the back of the book.

Writing Prompt

A. Read the questions carefully. Then circle the important words.

Which animals do you think make the best pets?

Why are they the best pets?

What can they do?

Write three reasons with details.

B. Think of your own best pets and write your answer. **Topic Sentence**

Q: Which animals do you think make the best pets?

I believe _____ make the best pets.

- cats - birds - hamsters - guinea pigs - rabbits
- turtles - lizards - snakes - fish

C. Ask and answer the following questions with your partner. Then add one more idea in each of the boxes. **Supporting Ideas**

Q: Why are these pets the best pets?

There **are** many kinds of **dogs** to choose from.

Choices

- cats
- birds
- hamsters
- guinea pigs
- rabbits
- turtles
- lizards
- snakes
- fish
- _____

Q: What is another thing that makes them good pets?

They **are** friendly and loyal.

Characteristics

- loving and playful
- soft and fuzzy
- sweet and lovable
- clean and intelligent
- interesting and quiet
- gentle and calm
- adorable and cute
- smart and a lot fun
- _____

Q: How hard is it to take care of these pets?

They **are** easy to take care of.

Pet Care

- easy to care for
- simple to take care of
- not very difficult to take care of
- not very hard to take care of
- _____

A. Talk about the pictures. Then read the story.

My Lovable Pet

Every kid needs a pet to care for, and I believe dogs are the best pets in the world. First of all, there are many kinds of dogs you can choose from. There are big dogs, small dogs, long-haired dogs, and short-haired dogs. Also, dogs come in many different colors. Second, dogs are friendly and loyal to their owners. They like to be with people, and they love to play with them. They protect people and their homes from dangers such as fire or a thief. Lastly, dogs are easy to take care of. They only need the right kind of food and fresh water. Also, you need to walk your dog every day. Dogs are wonderful, and everyone should have a dog as a pet.

B. Discuss the questions about the story.

- What does the boy think the best pets in the world are?
- What is his first reason?
- What is his second reason?
- What is his last reason?

Topic Sentence

dogs—the best pets in the world

Choices

many kinds
→ big, small, long-haired, and short-haired
→ many different colors

Characteristics

friendly and loyal
→ like to be with people
→ protect people and their homes

Pet Care

easy to take care of
→ the right kind of food and fresh water
→ walk them

Concluding Sentence

everyone should have a dog as a pet

Key Vocabulary & Expressions

- danger(s)
- long-haired, short-haired, loyal, fresh
- care for, believe/believed, choose/chose, protect/protected

Hunt for Sentence Parts

Read the story again and do as follows:

1. Draw circles on the subjects.
2. Draw rectangles on the verbs.
3. Draw stars on the objects.
4. Draw leaves on the complements.

Example I believe dogs are the best pets in the world.

Subject Ⓢ
Verb Ⓥ
Object Ⓞ
Complement Ⓒ

C. **Choose the best topic sentence for the picture.**

> **A** Cats meow and dogs bark.
>
> **B** I've never seen a dog in my life.
>
> **C** The best pets in the world are cats.
>
> **D** Dogs are the best pets in the world.

D. **Read the *Writing Sprouts* story again and write the details.**

1. There are many kinds of dogs you can choose from.

   There are big dogs, small dogs, long-haired dogs, and short-haired dogs .

   Also, dogs come in many different colors   .

2. Dogs are friendly and loyal to their owners.

   They _____.

   They _____.

3. Dogs are easy to take care of.

   They only need _____.

   Also, you need to _____.

Writing Process

Planning

Brainstorm and write your ideas. Any idea is all right. You can use the words and phrases on the *Writing Prompt* (pp. 42–43).

_____   _____

_____   _____

_____   _____

Topic
My Lovable Pet

Gathering & Organizing

Gather and organize your ideas in the correct boxes.

Topic: My Lovable Pet

Topic Sentence

Every kid needs a pet to care for, and I believe _____
are the best pets in the world.

Choices	Characteristics	Pet Care
There are many kinds of _____ you can choose from. _____ _____ _____.	They are _____ _____ _____ _____ _____ _____.	They are _____ _____ _____ _____ _____ _____.

Concluding Sentence

_____ are wonderful, and everyone should have _____.

Adding Your Own

Answer the questions below. You can write your own answers or choose from the examples in the box. Ideas and Details

Cats are the best pets because there are many kinds of cats to choose from. They come in many sizes and colors. You can choose one that is the best fit for your home.

Turtles are the best pets because there are many types of turtles you can choose from. They come in many different colors and sizes. You need to learn about each kind before you make your choice.

Cats are loving and playful. They like to be with people and play together. They are good companions.

Turtles are interesting and quiet. With their long necks and shells, they are wonderful to look at. They are good indoor pets because they are very quiet.

Cats are easy to care for. They only need the right kind of food and clean water. Also, they need cat toys to play with.

Turtles are not very difficult to take care of. You need to put them in the right-size cage. Also, you need to give them the proper food and fresh water every day.

Cats are wonderful, and everyone should have a cat as a pet.

Turtles are great, and everyone should have a turtle as a pet.

1. Why are these pets the best pets?

    _____

    _____

2. What is another thing that makes them good pets?

    _____

    _____

3. How hard is it to take care of these pets?

    _____

    _____

4. How do you feel about these pets?

    _____

    _____

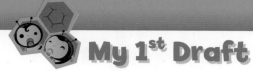 **My 1ˢᵗ Draft**

Rewrite your ideas from the previous pages in complete sentences.

Title	

My Lovable Pet

Topic Sentence

Every kid needs a pet to care for, and I believe
_____ are the best pets in the world.

Body

_____

_____

_____

_____

_____

_____

_____

_____

_____

_____

Concluding Sentence

_____

_____

✔**Peer Proofreading Checklist:**

☐ **Punctuation** ✔capitalization ✔commas(,) ✔periods(.) ✔question marks(?)
☐ **Correct spelling**
☐ **Complete sentences** S + V + end of sentence

Switch books with your partner and proofread your partner's writing.

↘ After proofreading your 1ˢᵗ draft, rewrite it on your final draft.

Fun Quiz

Q: Who is the dog on page 44 chasing?

A: The dog is chasing _____. <Answer Key p. 80>

Writing Prompt

A. Read the questions carefully. Then circle the important words.

Where did you go for your best vacation?

What did you do there?

Why was it your best vacation ever?

Write three reasons with details.

◀ **Topic Sentence**

B. Think of your own best vacation and write your answer.

Q: When was your best vacation, and where did you go?

_____, I went to _____, and

it was the best vacation I've ever had.

- Last summer, Last winter, Last year, Two years ago, Three years ago
- a museum, an art gallery, an arts center, an aquarium, an aquatic museum

C. Ask and answer the following questions with your partner. Then add one more idea in each of the boxes. **Supporting Ideas**

Q: What kinds of attractions did your vacation place have?

It **had** many fun rides.

Attractions

- many exhibitions
- many sea animals
- a lot of aquatic animals
- •

- all kinds of displays
- a variety of sea creatures
- so many kinds of marine life

Q: What events did it have?

It **had** fantastic shows.

Events

- amazing programs
- interesting programs
- fun activities
- educational programs
- •

- hands-on activities
- wonderful activities
- exciting events
- interactive programs

Q: What else was special about this place?

It **had** amazing gift shops.

Shopping

- nice gift shops
- awesome souvenir shops
- •

- cool gift stores

A. Talk about the pictures. Then read the story.

My Best Vacation

Last summer, my parents took me to Disneyland, and it was the best vacation I've ever had. First of all, Disneyland had many fun rides that we could choose from. It had roller coasters, boat rides, bumper cars, carousels, and much more. My favorite was a ride called Splash Mountain. Secondly, Disneyland had fantastic shows we could watch. There were several parades during the day, and we could see many fun Disney characters dancing to the music. At night, my family had a great time watching the exciting fireworks. Lastly, Disneyland had amazing gift shops. They sold T-shirts, toys, and candies. I bought an awesome key chain and a mouse-shaped lollipop there. I will never forget my best vacation to Disneyland.

B. Discuss the questions about the story.

- Where did the girl go for her best vacation?
- When did she go?
- What fun rides did the place have?
- What shows did the girl enjoy with her family?
- What did she buy at the gift shop?

Topic Sentence

last summer, the best vacation at Disneyland

Attractions

many fun rides
→ roller coasters, boat rides, bumper cars, carousels
→ Splash Mountain was my favorite

Events

fantastic shows
→ parades
→ fireworks

Shopping

amazing gift shops
→ T-shirts, toys, candies
→ bought a key chain and a lollipop

Concluding Sentence

will never forget my vacation

Key Vocabulary & Expressions

- vacation(s), ride(s), roller coaster(s), bumper car(s), carousel(s), parade(s), character(s), fireworks, lollipop(s)
- fantastic, amazing, awesome, mouse-shaped
- can/could, choose/chose, sell/sold, buy/bought

Hunt for Sentence Parts

Read the story again and do as follows:
1. Draw circles on the subjects.
2. Draw rectangles on the verbs.
3. Draw stars on the objects.
4. Draw leaves on the complements.

Example My parents took me to Disneyland.

Subject ⓢ
Verb ⓥ
Object ⓞ
Complement ⓒ

C. Choose the best topic sentence for the picture.

A You can see tigers and lions at an aquarium.

B I like museums, amusement parks, and aquariums.

C Last winter, my parents took me to a museum, and it was the best vacation ever.

D My family went on a vacation trip to an aquarium last summer.

D. Read the *Writing Sprouts* story again and write the details.

1. Disneyland had many fun rides that we could choose from.

   It had roller coasters, boat rides, bumper cars, carousels, and much more .

   My favorite was a ride called Splash Mountain   .

2. Disneyland had fantastic shows we could watch.

   During the day, there were _____ .

   At night, _____ .

3. Disneyland had amazing gift shops.

   They sold _____ .

   I bought _____ .

Writing Process

Planning

Brainstorm and write your ideas. Any idea is all right. You can use the words and phrases on the *Writing Prompt* (pp. 50–51).

Topic
My Best Vacation

Gathering & Organizing

Gather and organize your ideas in the correct boxes.

Topic: My Best Vacation

Topic Sentence

Last _____, my parents took me to _____, and it was the best vacation I've ever had.

Attractions	Events	Shopping
It had _____ _____. _____ _____.	It had _____ _____. _____ _____.	It had _____ _____. _____ _____.

Concluding Sentence

I will never forget my best vacation to _____.

Adding Your Own

Answer the questions below. You can write your own answers or choose from the examples in the box. Ideas and Details

The museum had many exhibitions. It had paintings, sculptures, and much more. My favorite was a painting of angels.

The aquarium had many sea animals. It had turtles, sharks, sea stars, and so many kinds of fish. My favorite was the jellyfish.

The museum had amazing programs. We got to join in the programs, and we could learn so many new things. My family had a great time doing hands-on activities.

The aquarium had wonderful activities. We got to join in some of the activities, and we could learn so much about underwater animals. My family had an exciting time feeding the sharks.

The museum had nice souvenir shops. They sold things such as books, posters, postcards, and magnets. I bought a book about the museum's paintings.

The aquarium had cool gift stores. They had neat things such as stuffed animals, books about sea animals, and magnets. I bought a nice octopus key chain.

I will never forget my best vacation to the museum.

I will never forget my best vacation to the aquarium.

1. What attractions did the place you visited have?

   _____

   _____

2. What events did it have?

   _____

   _____

3. What else was special about this place?

   _____

   _____

4. How do you feel about your best vacation ever?

   _____

   _____

My 1st Draft

Rewrite your ideas from the previous pages in complete sentences.

Title

> My Best Vacation

Topic Sentence

Last _____, my parents took me to _____,
and it was the best vacation I've ever had.

Body

Concluding Sentence

✔ **Peer Proofreading Checklist:**

☐ **Punctuation** ✔capitalization ✔commas(,) ✔periods(.) ✔question marks(?)
☐ **Correct spelling**
☐ **Complete sentences** S + V + end of sentence

> Switch books with your partner and proofread your partner's writing.

➤ After proofreading your 1st draft, rewrite it on your final draft.

Fun Quiz

Q: On page 52, what is the girl in the Disneyland gift shop wearing on her head?

A: She is wearing _____. <Answer Key p. 80>

How to Make a Great Sandwich

Writing Prompt

A. Read the questions carefully. Then circle the important words.

What kind of sandwiches do you like to eat? What are the ingredients? How do you make these sandwiches? Explain in detail how to make a sandwich that you like.

Topic Sentence

B. Think of your own favorite sandwiches and write your answer.

Q: What kind of sandwiches do you like to eat?

I | like | to eat _____.

- chicken sandwiches
- egg sandwiches

Q: What are the ingredients?

The ingredients | are | two pieces of bread, _____, mustard, mayonnaise, lettuce, tomatoes, and onions.

- chicken
- eggs

C. Ask and answer the following questions with your partner. Then add one more idea in each of the boxes. ◄ **Steps**

Q: How do you make your sandwiches?

First, **put** **some mustard and mayonnaise** on both pieces of the bread.

Step 1
- boil the chicken
- boil the eggs
- _____

Next, **put** **the ham** on one piece of the bread.

Step 2
- cut the chicken into little pieces
- chop the eggs into little pieces
- _____

Then, **lay** **the cheese** on the ham.

Step 3
- mix the chicken with mustard and mayonnaise
- mix the eggs with mayonnaise
- _____

After that, **add** **the vegetables.**

Step 4
- put the chicken with mustard and mayonnaise on one piece of the bread
- put the eggs with mayonnaise on one piece of the bread
- _____

Finally, **place** **the other piece of bread** on top of the stack.

Step 5
- add the vegetables and cheese
- place the vegetables and cheese on top
- _____

A. Talk about the pictures. Then read the story.

How to Make a Great Sandwich

I really love to eat ham-and-cheese sandwiches, and they are so easy to make. The ingredients are two pieces of bread, ham, cheese, mustard, mayonnaise, lettuce, tomatoes, and onions. First, put some mustard and mayonnaise on both pieces of the bread. You can use a knife to spread them around evenly. Next, put the ham on one piece of the bread. You can use one or two slices of ham. Then, lay the cheese on the ham. You can use one or two slices of cheese. After that, add the vegetables. You can use lettuce, tomato slices, and onion slices. Finally, place the other piece of bread on top of the stack. You can cut the sandwich into triangles with a knife. Enjoy your ham-and-cheese sandwich.

B. Discuss the questions about the story.

- What kind of sandwiches does the boy love to eat?
- What are the ingredients?
- What are the steps to make ham-and-cheese sandwiches?

Topic Sentence

love to eat ham-and-cheese sandwiches

Ingredients
two pieces of bread, ham, cheese, mustard, mayonnaise, lettuce, tomatoes, and onions

First
put mustard and mayonnaise on the bread

Next
put the ham

Then
lay the cheese

After that
add the vegetables

Finally
place the bread on top

Concluding Sentence

enjoy the sandwich

Key Vocabulary & Expressions

- sandwich(es), ingredient(s), piece(s), mustard, mayonnaise, lettuce, slice(s), vegetable(s), stack(s), triangle(s)
- spread/spread, lay/laid, add/added
- evenly

Hunt
for Sentence Parts

Read the story again and do as follows:
1. Draw circles on the subjects.
2. Draw rectangles on the verbs.
3. Draw stars on the objects.
4. Draw leaves on the complements.

Example I love to eat ham-and-cheese sandwiches.

Subject S
Verb V
Object O
Complement C

61

C. Choose the best topic sentence for the picture.

A Fried chicken is my favorite food.

B I love chicken sandwiches, and they are easy to make.

C I love boiled eggs, and you can eat them with salt.

D Egg sandwiches are my favorite, and it is very easy to make them.

D. Read the *Writing Sprouts* story again and write the details.

1. First, put some mustard and mayonnaise on both pieces of the bread.

   You can use a knife to spread them around evenly   .

2. Next, put the ham on one piece of the bread.

   You _____.

3. Then, lay the cheese on the ham.

   You _____.

4. After that, add the vegetables.

   You _____.

5. Finally, place the other piece of bread on top of the stack.

   You _____.

Writing Process

 **Planning**

Brainstorm and write your ideas. Any idea is all right. You can use the words and phrases on the *Writing Prompt* (pp. 58–59).

_____

_____

_____

Topic

How to Make
a Great Sandwich

 Gathering & Organizing

Gather and organize your ideas in the correct boxes.

Topic: How to Make a Great Sandwich

Topic Sentence

I really love to eat _____, and they are so easy to make.

Ingredients
_____
_____
_____
_____

First
_____
_____
_____

Next
_____
_____

Finally
_____
_____

After that
_____
_____

Then
_____
_____

Concluding Sentence

Now you can make _____ sandwiches for your family and friends.

Adding Your Own

Answer the questions below. You can write your own answers or choose from the examples in the box. Steps and Details

First, boil the chicken. You can use oven mitts to protect your hands from burning.

First, boil the eggs. You can use potholders to protect your hands from the heat.

Next, cut the chicken into little pieces. You need to use the knife carefully.

Next, chop the eggs into little pieces. You can use a knife to do this.

Then, mix the chicken with mustard and mayonnaise. You can use a spoon to mix them well.

Then, mix the eggs with mayonnaise. You need to mix them gently with a spoon.

After that, put the chicken on one piece of bread. You can use a knife or a spoon to spread the chicken evenly.

After that, put the eggs on one piece of bread. You can use a knife to spread the eggs evenly on the bread.

Finally, add the vegetables and cheese. You can put lettuce, tomato slices, and onion slices with the cheese. Place the other piece of bread on the top.

Finally, place the vegetables and cheese on the sandwich. You can add lettuce with tomato, onion, and cheese slices. Place the other piece of bread on the top.

Now you can make chicken/egg sandwiches for your family and friends.

1. What is the first step? _____

_____

2. What is the second step? _____

_____

3. What is the third step? _____

_____

4. What is the fourth step? _____

_____

5. What is the last step? _____

_____

6. What can you do for your family and friends?

_____

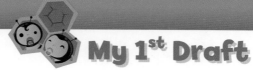

My 1st Draft

Rewrite your ideas from the previous pages in complete sentences.

Title

> # How to Make a Great Sandwich

Topic Sentence

I like to eat _____, and they are easy to make. The ingredients are _____

_____.

Body

Concluding Sentence

✔ **Peer Proofreading Checklist:**

- ☐ **Punctuation** ✔capitalization ✔commas(,) ✔periods(.) ✔question marks(?)
- ☐ **Correct spelling**
- ☐ **Complete sentences** S + V + end of sentence

Switch books with your partner and proofread your partner's writing.

➤ After proofreading your 1st draft, rewrite it on your final draft.

Fun Quiz

Q: On page 60, what is the shape of the sandwich the boy is holding?

A: It is _____. <Answer Key p. 80>

Writing Prompt

A. Read the questions carefully. Then circle the important words.

If you could travel to another planet,

which planet would you go to?

What is special about the planet?

Write three reasons with details.

Topic Sentence

B. Think of a planet you would like to go to and write your answer.

Q: Which planet would you go to, and what do you know about the planet?

I | would go | to _____ .

It | is _____ .

- Jupiter, Saturn
- the fifth planet from the Sun   • the sixth planet from the Sun
- the largest planet in the solar system
- the second-largest planet in the solar system

C. Ask and answer the following questions with your partner. Then add one more idea in each of the boxes. Supporting Ideas

Q: What is special about the planet you chose?

It   has   Olympus Mons,   the tallest mountain in the solar system.

- the Great Red Spot   • a huge ring system
- _____

Features

Q: How strong is the gravity on the planet?

The gravity on this planet   is **not**   as strong as the gravity on Earth.

- greater than the gravity on Earth
- similar to the gravity on Earth
- 2.4 times stronger than the gravity on Earth
- about 1.07 times Earth's gravity
- _____

Gravity

Q: How many moons does the planet have?

It   has   two moons.

- at least sixty-seven moons   • more than sixty moons
- many moons orbiting it
- lots of moons in orbit around it
- _____

Moons

A. Talk about the pictures. Then read the story.

Travel to Another Planet

If I could travel to another planet, I would go to Mars, the fourth planet from the Sun. The first reason is because Mars has Olympus Mons, the tallest mountain in the solar system. It is three times taller than Mount Everest. I want to be the first person to climb to the top of the mountain. The second reason is because the gravity on Mars is not as strong as the gravity on Earth. A person can jump three times higher on Mars than on Earth. I want to jump around on Mars. The last reason is because Mars has two moons. Their names are Phobos and Deimos, and they orbit Mars. I want to enjoy watching the two moons in the sky. I wish my dream of going to Mars would come true.

B. Discuss the questions about the story.

- Which planet would the girl go to?
- Where is the planet located in the solar system?
- What is on Mars?
- How strong is the gravity on Mars?
- How many moons does Mars have?

Topic Sentence

I would go to Mars, the fourth planet from the Sun.

Features

Olympus Mons
→ taller than Mount Everest
→ want to climb

Gravity

not as strong
→ can jump three times higher
→ want to jump around

Moons

two moons
→ Phobos and Deimos
→ want to enjoy watching them

Concluding Sentence

I wish my dream of going to Mars would come true.

Key Vocabulary & Expressions

- planet(s), Mars, solar system(s), Mount Everest, gravity, moon(s)
- travel/traveled, climb/climbed, orbit/orbited, enjoy/enjoyed, wish/wished
- four/fourth

Hunt for Sentence Parts

Read the story again and do as follows:
1. Draw circles on the subjects.
2. Draw rectangles on the verbs.
3. Draw stars on the objects.
4. Draw leaves on the complements.

Example The first reason is because Mars has Olympus Mons.

Subject Ⓢ
Verb Ⓥ
Object Ⓞ
Complement Ⓒ

69

C. Choose the best topic sentence for the picture.

A Many aliens live on Mars, the biggest planet in our solar system.

B I want to travel to Mars, the second-smallest planet in the solar system.

C Jupiter is the smallest planet in our solar system.

D If I could travel to another planet, I would go to Jupiter.

D. Read the *Writing Sprouts* story again and write the details.

1. Mars has Olympus Mons, the tallest mountain in the solar system.

   It is three times taller than Mount Everest .

   I want to be the first person to climb to the top of the mountain .

2. The gravity on Mars is not as strong as the gravity on Earth.

   A person _____ .

   I _____ .

3. Mars has two moons.

   Their names are _____ .

   I _____ .

Planning

Brainstorm and write your ideas. Any idea is all right. You can use the words and phrases on the *Writing Prompt* (pp. 66–67).

Topic
Travel to Another Planet

Gathering & Organizing

Gather and organize your ideas in the correct boxes.

Topic: Travel to Another Planet

Topic Sentence

If I could travel to another planet, I would go to _____,
the _____ planet from the Sun.

Features	Gravity	Moons
It has _____	The gravity is _____	It has _____
_____.	_____.	_____.
_____	_____	_____
_____.	_____.	_____.

Concluding Sentence

I wish my dream of going to _____ would come true.

Adding Your Own

Answer the questions below. You can write your own answers or choose from the examples in the box. ◄ **Ideas and Details**

Jupiter has the Great Red Spot. The Great Red Spot is a huge storm, and it has been blowing for over 300 years. I want to feel the power of the storm.

Saturn has a huge ring system. Saturn's rings are made of pieces of ice and rock. I want to see the beautiful rings up close.

The gravity on Jupiter is greater than the gravity on Earth. I would weigh two and a half times as much as I do on Earth. I want to feel the strong pull of gravity.

The gravity on Saturn is similar to the gravity on Earth. I would feel as if I am on Earth. I want to move around freely on Saturn.

Jupiter has at least sixty-seven moons. Jupiter's largest moon is Ganymede, and it is the largest moon in the solar system. I want to see how big it is up close.

Saturn has more than sixty moons. Saturn's largest moon is Titan. I want to know how it feels to see so many moons in the sky.

I wish my dream of going to Jupiter would come true.

I wish my dream of going to Saturn would come true.

1. What special feature does the planet have?

   _____

   _____

2. How strong is the gravity on the planet?

   _____

   _____

3. How many moons does the planet have?

   _____

   _____

4. What do you wish about the planet?

   _____

   _____

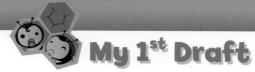

My 1st Draft

Rewrite your ideas from the previous pages in complete sentences.

Title

Topic Sentence

Body

Concluding Sentence

| Travel to Another Planet |

If I could travel to another planet, I would go to _____
_____ , the _____ planet from the Sun.

✔ **Peer Proofreading Checklist:**

☐ **Punctuation** ✔capitalization ✔commas(,) ✔periods(.) ✔question marks(?)
☐ **Correct spelling**
☐ **Complete sentences** S + V + end of sentence

Switch books with your partner and proofread your partner's writing.

↳ After proofreading your 1st draft, rewrite it on your final draft.

Fun Quiz

Q: On page 68, what planet can you see next to Mars?

A: I can see _____ . <Answer Key p. 80>

Review Units 5 & 6

A. Write the past tense.

1. take _____

2. see _____

3. sell _____

4. buy _____

5. need _____

6. choose _____

7. believe _____

8. come _____

9. like _____

10. protect _____

B. Complete the topic and concluding sentences using the phrases from the box below.

1. Every kid needs a pet _____

_____.

2. I will never forget _____

_____.

3. Last summer, my parents took me to Disneyland, _____

_____.

4. Dogs are wonderful, _____

_____.

- and everyone should have a dog as a pet
- my best vacation to Disneyland
- to care for, and I believe dogs are the best pets in the world
- and it was the best vacation I've ever had

C. Write the proper supporting ideas from the box below.

1. _____

They sold T-shirts, toys, and candies. I bought an awesome key chain and a mouse-shaped lollipop there.

2. _____

They only need the right kind of food and fresh water. Also, you need to walk your dog every day.

3. _____

It had roller coasters, boat rides, bumper cars, carousels, and much more. My favorite was a ride called Splash Mountain.

4. _____

There are big dogs, small dogs, long-haired dogs, and short-haired dogs. Also, dogs come in many different colors.

5. _____

They like to be with people, and they love to play with them. They protect people and their homes from dangers such as fire or a thief.

6. _____

There were several parades during the day, and we could see many fun Disney characters dancing to the music. At night, my family had a great time watching the exciting fireworks.

- Secondly, Disneyland had fantastic shows we could watch.
- Lastly, dogs are easy to take care of.
- First of all, there are many kinds of dogs you can choose from.
- Second, dogs are friendly and loyal to their owners.
- First of all, Disneyland had many fun rides that we could choose from.
- Lastly, Disneyland had amazing gift shops.

 Activity cards are available at the back of the book.

Review Units 7 & 8

A. Write the past tense.

1. travel _____
2. jump _____
3. come true _____
4. use _____
5. add _____

6. want _____
7. put _____
8. spread _____
9. lay _____
10. place _____

B. Complete the topic and concluding sentences using the phrases from the box below.

1. Enjoy _____

_____.

2. If I could travel to another planet, _____

_____.

3. I really love to eat ham-and-cheese sandwiches, _____

_____.

4. I wish _____

_____.

- your ham-and-cheese sandwich
- my dream of going to Mars would come true
- and they are so easy to make
- I would go to Mars, the fourth planet from the Sun

C. Write the proper supporting ideas from the box below.

1. _____

   It is three times taller than Mount Everest. I want to be the first person to climb to the top of the mountain.

2. _____

   You can use a knife to spread them around evenly.

3. _____

   You can cut the sandwich into triangles with a knife.

4. _____

   Their names are Phobos and Deimos, and they orbit Mars. I want to enjoy watching the two moons in the sky.

5. _____

   You can use one or two slices of cheese. After that, add the vegetables. You can use lettuce, tomato slices, and onion slices.

6. _____

   A person can jump three times higher on Mars than on Earth. I want to jump around on Mars.

- The last reason is because Mars has two moons.
- Then, lay the cheese on the ham.
- Finally, place the other piece of bread on top of the stack.
- The second reason is because the gravity on Mars is not as strong as the gravity on Earth.
- First, put some mustard and mayonnaise on both pieces of the bread.
- The first reason is because Mars has Olympus Mons, the tallest mountain in the solar system.

 Activity cards are available at the back of the book.

Writing Help

 ## Past Tense — Regular Verbs

most verbs + -ed	learn → learned	watch → watched
after -e + -d	live → lived	dance → danced
consonant + -y → -ied **vowel + -y → -ed**	cry → cried play → played	study → studied enjoy → enjoyed
one vowel + one consonant → double consonant + -ed	stop → stopped	plan → planned

 ## Past Tense — Irregular Verbs

Now	In the Past	Now	In the Past	Now	In the Past
am, is	was	forget	forgot	run	ran
are	were	get	got	see	saw
buy	bought	give	gave	sell	sold
can	could	go	went	spread	spread
choose	chose	lay	laid	swim	swam
come	came	make	made	take	took
do	did	put	put	teach	taught
eat	ate	read	read	tell	told
fall	fell	ride	rode	will	would

 ## Comparatives and Superlatives

most adjectives / adverbs + -er / est	strong, stronger, strongest high, higher, highest
after -e + -r / st	large, larger, largest
consonant + -y → -ier / iest	dirty, dirtier, dirtiest
one vowel + one consonant → double consonant + -er / est	big, bigger, biggest

Transition Words and Phrases

Sequencing ideas	Showing time
first (of all) / second / third the first reason is… after / before (we arrived home) afterward at first at last before long as soon as (we finished our homework) finally later next after that soon then	now today tomorrow yesterday last week / this week / next week last year / this year / next year suddenly during (my summer vacation) until (I was ten years old) when (we go on a picnic) (five years) ago at (one o'clock) in the morning / in the afternoon / in the evening / at night
Adding ideas	**Concluding a paragraph**
another example is that… another reason is that… also in addition / besides too	finally lastly in conclusion in summary

 Common Spelling Mistakes

their there	they're(=they are)	see	sea	then	than	
your	you're(=you are)	write	right	two	too	to
its	it's (=it is)	hear	here	four	for	
whose	who's (=who is)	meet	meat	dear	deer	
wear	where	buy	by	quiet	quite	

Answer Key

Unit 1 My Best Birthday Ever ▶p.13

Fun Quiz: What are the three kids on page 8 eating?
A: They are eating popcorn.

Unit 2 My Favorite Food ▶p.21

Fun Quiz: What kind of pizza is the boy on page 16 eating?
A: He is eating a piece of combination pizza.

Unit 3 Aunt Lucy, My Hero ▶p.29

Fun Quiz: What color is Andrew's bicycle on page 24?
A: It is red and black.

Unit 4 My Favorite Room ▶p.37

Fun Quiz: What color is the girl's blanket on page 32?
A: It is orange.

Unit 5 My Lovable Pet ▶p.49

Fun Quiz: Who is the dog on page 44 chasing?
A: The dog is chasing a thief.

Unit 6 My Best Vacation ▶p.57

Fun Quiz: On page 52, what is the girl in the Disneyland gift shop wearing on her head?
A: She is wearing a Minnie Mouse hat.

Unit 7 How to Make a Great Sandwich ▶p.65

Fun Quiz: On page 60, what is the shape of the sandwich the boy is holding?
A: It is a triangle.

Unit 8 Travel to Another Planet ▶p.73

Fun Quiz: On page 68, what planet can you see next to Mars?
A: I can see the Earth.

Subject	Verb	Complement
I (s)	**go(es) / went** (v)	to the movies with friends.
He / She (s)	**run(s) / ran** (v)	behind me to help me balance at the park.
There (s)	**are / were** (v)	several parades during the day. (s)
I (s)	**fall(s) / fell** (v)	so many times.
My dad / mom (s)	**is / was** (v)	a great mentor. (c)
My room (s)	**is / was** (v)	a very special place to me in my home. (c)
Dogs (s)	**are / were** (v)	friendly and loyal. (c)

Writing Garden Book 2

Writing Garden Book 2

Writing Garden Book 2

Writing Garden Book 2

Writing Garden Book 2

Writing Garden Book 2

Writing Garden Book 2

Writing Garden Book 2

Writing Garden Book 2

Writing Garden Book 2

Writing Garden Book 2

Writing Garden Book 2

Writing Garden Book 2

Writing Garden Book 2

Writing Garden Book 2

Writing Garden Book 2

Writing Garden Book 2

Writing Garden Book 2

(s)	(v)	
I	am / was	(c) happy because of many wonderful events.
Dogs	are / were	(c) easy to take care of.
My favorite	is / was	(c) a ride called Splash Mountain.
We	can make / could make	(★) many kinds of pizza with the toppings.
They	think(s) / thought	(★) pizza is the best food in the world.
My aunt / uncle	take(s) / took	(★) me to the library every weekend.
Mom/Dad	will have / would have	(★) a special place in my heart.

Writing Garden Book 2

Writing Garden Book 2

Writing Garden Book 2

Writing Garden Book 2

Writing Garden Book 2

Writing Garden Book 2

Writing Garden Book 2

Writing Garden Book 2

Writing Garden Book 2

Writing Garden Book 2

Writing Garden Book 2

Writing Garden Book 2

Writing Garden Book 2

Writing Garden Book 2

Writing Garden Book 2

Writing Garden Book 2

Writing Garden Book 2

Writing Garden Book 2

S	V	
I	love(s) / loved	to be in my soft bed on a rainy day.
We	believe(s) / believed	dogs are the best pets in the world.
Everyone	should have	a dog as a pet.
We	will never forget	our best vacation to Disneyland.
My family	have (has) / had	a great time watching the exciting fireworks.
You	can cut / could cut	the sandwich into triangles with a knife.
Every kid	need(s) / needed	a pet to care for.

Writing Garden Book 2

Writing Garden Book 2

Writing Garden Book 2

Writing Garden Book 2

Writing Garden Book 2

Writing Garden Book 2

Writing Garden Book 2

Writing Garden Book 2

Writing Garden Book 2

Writing Garden Book 2

Writing Garden Book 2

Writing Garden Book 2

Writing Garden Book 2

Writing Garden Book 2

Writing Garden Book 2

Writing Garden Book 2

Writing Garden Book 2

Writing Garden Book 2

S	V	
My aunt / uncle	show(s) / showed	me how important it is to read books. (I.O / D.O)
Mom/Dad	teach(es) / taught	me to be brave. (I.O / D.O)
You	teach(es) / taught	me how to ride a bicycle. (I.O / D.O)
My teacher	help(s) / helped	me to make friends. (I.O / O.C)
Pizza	make(s) / made	me strong and healthy. (I.O / O.C)
You	encourage(s) / encouraged	me to read many kinds of books. (I.O / O.C)
She	tell(s) / told	me to study. (I.O / O.C)

Writing Garden Book 2

Writing Garden Book 2

Writing Garden Book 2

Writing Garden Book 2

Writing Garden Book 2

Writing Garden Book 2

Writing Garden Book 2

Writing Garden Book 2

Writing Garden Book 2

Writing Garden Book 2

Writing Garden Book 2

Writing Garden Book 2

Writing Garden Book 2

Writing Garden Book 2

Writing Garden Book 2

Writing Garden Book 2

Writing Garden Book 2

Writing Garden Book 2

Writing Garden Book 2

Writing Garden Book 2

Writing Garden Book 2

Review Stickers

▶ page 39

▶ page 41

▶ page 75

▶ page 77

Writing Garden

Workbook 2

J. Randolph Lewis
Lucy Han
Helen Kim

Paragraph Writing

What are drones, and what can they
are like flying robots.

Writing Garden 2
Written by J. Randolph Lewis, Lucy Han, Helen Kim

Publisher: Anna Park

Project Director: Lucy Han

Content Editor: Kelli Ripatti, Sherry Lee

Designer: Eun Jee Kang

Illustrators: Beehive Illustration (Beatrice Bencivenni, John Lund, Philip Hailstone)

Cover Design: Hongdangmoo

Printer: Kyujang TPC

ISBN: 979-11-87999-00-3
Photo Credits:
Photos and images © Shutterstock, Inc.

www.runningturtle.co.kr
1203, 36, Hwangsaeul-ro 200beon-gil, Bundang-gu, Seongnam-si, Gyeonggi-do, KOREA 13595
TEL: +82-2-3452-7979 FAX: +82-31-718-3452

KC This book has been printed with non-toxic materials.

Writing Garden

Workbook 2

My Best Birthday Ever

🌱 Sentence Practice

A. Rewrite the sentences using the past tense.

Q: Where did you go on your birthday?

I **went** to a park on my birthday last weekend.
Past Tense

1. We go to an amusement park on my birthday.

   We went to an amusement park on my birthday last year .

2. I go to a theme park on my birthday.

   _____ last Sunday.

3. He goes to a zoo on his birthday.

   _____ last weekend.

4. She goes to a shopping mall on her birthday.

   _____ last month.

5. They go to a department store on Parents' Day.

   _____ last year.

6. My family goes to a movie theater for my brother's birthday.

   _____ last night.

7. John goes to a family restaurant on his birthday.

   _____ last spring.

8. Sue goes to Europe on her birthday.

   _____ last summer.

B. Rewrite the sentences using the past tense.

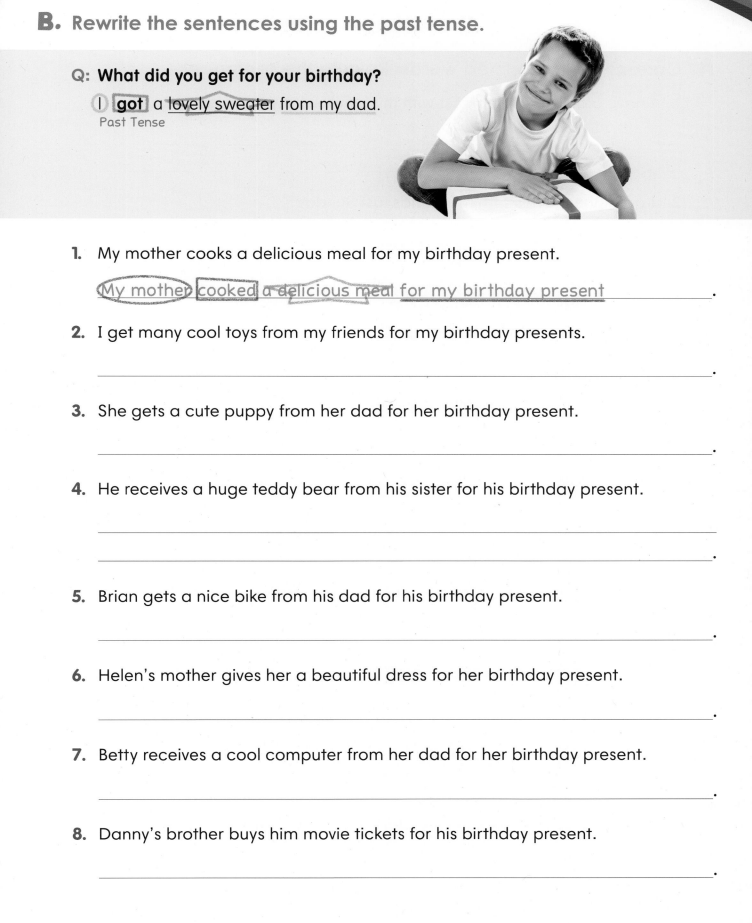

Q: What did you get for your birthday?

I got a lovely sweater from my dad.
Past Tense

1. My mother cooks a delicious meal for my birthday present.

   My mother cooked a delicious meal for my birthday present   .

2. I get many cool toys from my friends for my birthday presents.

   _____.

3. She gets a cute puppy from her dad for her birthday present.

   _____.

4. He receives a huge teddy bear from his sister for his birthday present.

   _____

   _____.

5. Brian gets a nice bike from his dad for his birthday present.

   _____.

6. Helen's mother gives her a beautiful dress for her birthday present.

   _____.

7. Betty receives a cool computer from her dad for her birthday present.

   _____.

8. Danny's brother buys him movie tickets for his birthday present.

   _____.

3

A. Correct the underlined words. Rewrite the sentences.

1. I <u>have</u> a delicious breakfast with my family on my last birthday.

    _____

    _____ .

2. I <u>go</u> to the movies with my friends last Sunday.

    _____

    _____ .

3. I really enjoyed the movie, <u>but</u> the popcorn was yummy.

    _____

    _____ .

4. <u>in</u> the evening, we watched a movie.

    _____

    _____ .

B. Expand the sentences below by adding the correct phrases from the box.

- with a red bow on his head
- with my family
- with my friends

- with red and blue lenses
- with strawberries and whipped cream on top

---

1. It was a cute little puppy <u>with a red bow on his head</u>_____ .

2. My mom made waffles _____ .

3. In the morning, I had a delicious breakfast _____ .

4. In the afternoon, I went to the movies _____ .

5. It was a 3-D movie, and we all put on special glasses _____

    _____ .

My Final Draft

Title: My Best Birthday Ever

My _____ birthday was the best birthday ever,

and I was _____ .

_____

_____

_____

_____

_____

_____

_____

_____

_____

_____

_____

_____

_____

_____

<More Than 120 Words>

My Comment ☐ Good
☐ Excellent

Parent's Comment ☐ Good ☐ Excellent
Teacher's Comment ☐ Good ☐ Excellent

5

🌱 Sentence Practice

A. Combine the words or phrases using *and*.

Q: What toppings do you like on your pizza?

I like <u>vegetables</u> on my pizza.   +   I like <u>chicken</u> on my pizza.

➡ I like <u>vegetables</u> **and** <u>chicken</u> on my pizza.
   Connecting Word

1. Pizza makes me <u>strong</u>. Pizza makes me <u>healthy</u>.

   Pizza makes me strong and healthy   .

2. Fried chicken is <u>crispy</u>. Fried chicken is <u>crunchy</u>.

   _____ .

3. <u>The pasta</u> has a lot of nutrients. <u>The sauce</u> has a lot of nutrients.

   _____ have _____ .

4. <u>The tomato sauce</u> on the crust is fantastic. <u>The cheese</u> on the crust is fantastic.

   _____ are _____ .

5. <u>Pizza</u> is an Italian food. <u>Pasta</u> is an Italian food.

   _____ are _____ .

6. Chicken with <u>seasonings</u> is wonderful. Chicken with <u>spices</u> is wonderful.

   _____ .

7. <u>Mushrooms</u> are popular toppings. <u>Onions</u> are popular toppings.

   _____ .

8. I love <u>fried chicken</u>. I love <u>French fries</u>.

   _____ .

B. Combine the two sentences using *because*.

Q: What is your favorite food and why do you like it?

I love <u>pizza</u>. + I can put different toppings on <u>pizza</u>.

→ I ⬚love⬚ pizza **because** I can put different toppings on **it**.

  Connecting Word

1. My favorite food is <u>pizza</u>. I can put different toppings on <u>pizza</u>.

   <u>My favorite food is pizza because I can put different toppings on it</u>.

2. I love to eat <u>fried chicken</u>. <u>Fried chicken</u> is so delicious.

   _____.

3. I like <u>pasta</u>. <u>Pasta</u> is so tasty.

   _____.

4. I love <u>spaghetti</u>. I can put different kinds of sauces on <u>the spaghetti</u>.

   _____

   _____.

5. <u>Fried chicken</u> is great. <u>Fried chicken</u> is nutritious and delicious.

   _____

   _____.

6. I like <u>fried chicken</u>. I can put many seasonings and spices on <u>fried chicken</u>.

   _____

   _____.

7. <u>Chicken</u> is good for children. <u>Chicken</u> has lots of protein.

   _____

   _____.

8. Please don't put <u>pepperoni</u> on the pizza. I don't like <u>pepperoni</u>.

   _____

   _____.

7

Revising Practice

A. Correct the underlined words. Rewrite the sentences.

1. She <u>can makes</u> many kinds of spaghetti with the sauces.

   _____ .

2. Spaghetti <u>make</u> me strong and healthy.

   _____ .

3. My favorite food is fried chicken <u>so</u> it is so tasty.

   _____ .

4. Some popular <u>topping</u> are pepperoni, mushrooms, onions, and cheese.

   _____ .

B. Expand the sentences below by adding the correct phrases from the box.

> • crispy and crunchy
> • different seasonings and tasty spices
> • with pepperoni, mushrooms, onions, and cheese toppings

1. I can put seasonings and spices on the chicken.

   → _I can put different seasonings and tasty spices on the chicken_ .

2. My mom can cook fried chicken.

   → _____ .

3. His favorite food is yummy pizza.

   → _____ .

My Final Draft

Title: My Favorite Food

My favorite food is _____, and it is

_____ .

_____

_____

_____

_____

_____

_____

_____

_____

_____

_____

_____

_____

_____

_____

_____

<More Than 120 Words>

My Comment ☐ Good ☐ Excellent

Parent's Comment ☐ Good ☐ Excellent
Teacher's Comment ☐ Good ☐ Excellent

🌱 Sentence Practice

A. Rewrite the sentences using the past tense.

Q: What did she/he do for you?

She **explained** the rules of the game to me.

I **could learn** the rules of the game from her.

Past Tense

1. You help me to make good friends.

   You helped me to make good friends   .

2. She shows me how important it is to read books.

   _____ .

3. He encourages me to read many kinds of books.

   _____ .

4. You tell me to study hard.

   _____ .

5. My mom teaches me to be brave.

   _____ .

6. My aunt takes me to the library.

   _____ .

7. I can learn many things from Uncle Kevin.

   _____ .

8. She runs behind me to help me balance.

   _____ .

B. Put the words in the correct order.

She taught me how to ride a bike.
To Whom   What

1. how to balance / me / taught

   Aunt Lucy taught me how to balance   .

2. told / what to read / me/

   My grandfather   .

3. taught / how to play baseball / me

   He   .

4. what good manners are / me / showed

   Anna   .

5. taught / me / how to play the piano

   John   .

6. showed / how to cook delicious hot dogs / me

   My mom   .

7. me / to read many books / told

   You   .

8. when to start / told / me

   My uncle   .

 **Revising Practice**

A. Correct the underlined words. Rewrite the sentences.

1. <u>at</u> the park, you ran behind me to help me balance.

   _____

   _____.

2. You <u>take</u> me to the library and encouraged me to read many books.

   _____

   _____.

3. I was shy and didn't have any friends, <u>because</u> you taught me to be brave.

   _____

   _____.

4. You will always <u>has</u> a special place in my heart.

   _____

   _____.

B. Expand the sentences below by adding the correct phrases from the box.

> • when I was so scared in the dark at night
> • at the library near my house
> • and showed me how to move my arms and legs in the water

1. He encouraged me to read many books. ↝ Add where.

   He encouraged me to read many books at the library near my house .

2. She taught me how to swim. ↝ Add more about how.

   _____

   _____.

3. My dad helped me to be brave and strong. ↝ Add when.

   _____

   _____.

My Final Draft

Title: _____ **, My Hero**

Dear _____ ,

You are my hero, and you are _____

_____ .

_____

_____

_____

_____

_____

_____

_____

_____

_____

_____

_____

_____

_____

_____

_____

_____

<More Than 130 Words>

My Comment ☐ Good
☐ Excellent

Parent's Comment ☐ Good ☐ Excellent
Teacher's Comment ☐ Good ☐ Excellent

🌱 Sentence Practice

A. Combine two sentences.

Q: **What do you have in your room?**

My room has a bed. The bed is near the window.

→ My room has a bed near the window.

1. My room has a comfortable armchair. The comfortable armchair is by the wall.

   My room has a comfortable armchair by the wall _____ .

2. My bed has a warm blanket. The blanket is on top of it.

   _____ .

3. My room has a computer. The computer is on my desk.

   _____ .

4. My room has a desk. The desk is in front of the window.

   _____ .

5. My room has a huge teddy bear. The huge teddy bear is next to the bed.

   _____ .

6. Our living room has a big-screen TV. The big-screen TV is by the sofa.

   _____ .

7. My room has a beautiful picture. The beautiful picture is on the wall.

   _____ .

8. I have lots of toys. The toys are in the toy box.

   _____ .

B. Choose the correct words and complete the sentences.

Q: What is your house like?

The living room **is** comfortable.

The living room **has** a comfortable sofa.

1. The room is (small but very comfortable / a small bed and a comfortable armchair).

   The room is small but very comfortable_____.

2. My room has (cozy and fancy / a fancy computer) on the desk.

   _____.

3. The teddy bear is (a bow around its neck / brown and huge).

   _____.

4. There is (a comfortable gray sofa / brown and comfortable) in the living room.

   _____.

5. There is (special and happy / a special and happy place) for my family.

   _____.

6. My sister has lots of (interesting / interesting books) in her room.

   _____.

7. My bedroom is (safe and comfortable / a cozy bed and a huge teddy bear).

   _____.

8. My dream house has (huge and beautiful / a huge living room).

   _____.

 **Revising Practice**

A. Correct the underlined words. Rewrite the sentences.

1. I love my room because it is cozy, and there <u>is</u> three things that make it so nice.

   _____

   _____.

2. I love to be in my soft bed <u>in</u> a rainy day.

   _____.

3. The computer is on my desk, and <u>they are</u> very useful.

   _____.

4. I always hug my teddy bear when I <u>was</u> sad.

   _____.

B. Expand the sentences below by adding the correct phrases from the box.

> • on my desk in front of the window   • small, soft, comfortable
> • when I am sad or tired

1. A bed is in my room. ➤ Describe the bed using more details.

   <u>A small, soft, comfortable bed is in my room</u>   .

2. I love to hug my teddy bear. ➤ Add when.

   _____.

3. My room has a fancy computer. ➤ Add where.

   _____

   _____.

Title: My Favorite Room

_____ is the best place in my home because
it is _____. There are three things that
make it so nice.

_____

_____

_____

_____

_____

_____

_____

_____

_____

_____

_____

_____

_____

_____

<More Than 130 Words>

My Comment	☐ Good		Parent's Comment	☐ Good	☐ Excellent
	☐ Excellent		Teacher's Comment	☐ Good	☐ Excellent

🌱 Sentence Practice

A. Complete the sentences using *need to* or *don't need to*.

> **Q: What do you need to do?**
> You **need to walk** your dog every day.
> You **don't need to wash** your dog every week.

1. Dogs want to love and be loved.

   You _____ need to _____ give them a lot of love.

2. Cats are clean animals, and they can clean themselves.

   You _____ wash your cat.

3. Goldfish only need a small tank.

   You _____ buy a big fish tank.

4. Dogs love to play with people.

   You _____ understand that your dog wants to spend time with you.

5. Things you say or do to your dog can make it happy or sad.

   You _____ understand that dogs have feelings like people.

6. Dogs love to be outside.

   You _____ take them out for a walk.

7. Dogs are very smart. You can teach your dog to do tricks.

   You _____ give your dog snacks when you train it.

8. Parrots learn how to talk just by listening to people talk.

   You _____ train your parrot to talk.

B. Choose the correct words and rewrite the sentences.

Q: Are there many kinds of dogs?
Yes. **There** are many kinds of dogs.

Q: What are dogs like?
They are loyal and friendly.

1. (There are / They are) many types of turtles you can choose from.

   There are many types of turtles you can choose from   .

2. I like turtles. (There are / They are) fun to watch.

   _____.

3. (There are / They are) long-haired dogs and short-haired dogs in the pet shop.

   _____.

4. I love cats because (there are / they are) easy to care for.

   _____.

5. Turtles are quiet. (There are / They are) good indoor pets.

   _____.

6. (There are / They are) different kinds of food you can buy for your cat.

   _____.

7. I have two cats. (There are / They are) loving and playful.

   _____.

8. (There are / They are) turtles in many different sizes in the pet shop.

   _____.

A. Correct the underlined words. Rewrite the sentences.

1. I believe dogs <u>is</u> the best pets in the world.

   _____.

2. Dogs <u>likes</u> to be with people.

   _____.

3. I love dogs because there <u>is</u> many kinds of dogs to choose from.

   _____.

4. They <u>protects</u> people and their homes from danger.

   _____.

B. Expand the sentences below by adding the correct phrases from the box.

> • and they want to belong to a family
> • when someone tries to hurt them
> • because they want to love and be loved

1. Dogs like to be with people. ➤ Add why.

   <u>Dogs like to be with people because they want to love and be loved</u>   .

2. Dogs protect their owners. ➤ Add when.

   _____

   _____.

3. Dogs are friendly and loyal. ➤ Add more about their characteristics.

   _____

   _____.

Title: My Lovable Pet

Every kid needs a pet to care for, and I believe
_____ are the best pets in the world.

_____

_____

_____

_____

_____

_____

_____

_____

_____

_____

_____

_____

_____

_____

_____

<More Than 140 Words>

My Comment ☐ Good
☐ Excellent

Parent's Comment ☐ Good ☐ Excellent
Teacher's Comment ☐ Good ☐ Excellent

🌱 Sentence Practice

A. Choose the correct verb and rewrite the sentences.

Q: What was there to see and do in Disneyland?
There **were** many fun rides **in Disneyland**.
Disneyland **had** many fun rides.

1. There (had / were) roller coasters, boat rides, bumper cars, and much more.

   <u>There were roller coasters, boat rides, bumper cars, and much more</u> .

2. The park (was / had) a ride called Splash Mountain.

   _____ .

3. There (were / had) several parades during the day, and we enjoyed the shows.

   _____
   _____ .

4. Disneyland also (was / had) fantastic shows we could enjoy.

   _____ .

5. At night, there (were / had) several shows in the park.

   _____ .

6. The aquarium (were / had) wonderful activities.

   _____ .

7. There (was / had) a cool gift shop in the aquarium.

   _____ .

8. The museum (were / had) wonderful paintings and sculptures.

   _____ .

B. Rewrite the sentences using the past tense.

Q: **Where did your family go last summer?**

We went to Disneyland.
Past Tense

1. My family goes to the Louvre Museum in Paris.

   My family went to the Louvre Museum in Paris last summer .

2. My uncle takes us to the Statue of Liberty in New York.

   _____ last winter.

3. My family visits my aunt's family in Spain.

   _____ last month.

4. We can see fantastic fireworks.

   _____ last night.

5. We visit Universal Studios Hollywood and have a great time there.

   _____

   _____ in 2016.

6. I buy an awesome key chain in the gift shop.

   _____ last summer.

7. My aunt takes us to the Sydney Opera House and shows us the famous building.

   _____

   _____ two years ago.

8. The museum gift shop sells nice paintings.

   _____ last year.

Revising Practice

A. Correct the underlined words. Rewrite the sentences.

1. There were several <u>parade</u> during the day.

    _____.

2. We <u>could saw</u> many wonderful Disney characters dancing to the music.

    _____.

3. My family <u>has</u> a great time watching the fireworks last year.

    _____.

4. Last summer, my parents <u>take</u> me to Disneyland.

    _____.

B. Expand the sentences below by adding the correct phrases from the box.

> - in the main gift shop near the entrance
> - that lit up in the sky with wonderful lights and colors
> - because it was a fun and exciting water ride

1. My favorite was a ride called Splash Mountain. ⇝ Add why.

    <u>My favorite was a ride called Splash Mountain because it was a fun and</u>
    <u>exciting water ride</u>_____.

2. My family had a great time watching the fireworks.

    ⇝ Add more about fireworks.

    _____

    _____.

3. I bought an awesome key chain and a mouse-shaped lollipop. ⇝ Add where.

    _____

    _____.

Title: My Best Vacation

Last _____ , my parents took me to

_____ , and it was the best vacation I've ever had.

_____

_____

_____

_____

_____

_____

_____

_____

_____

_____

_____

_____

_____

_____

_____

_____

<More Than 140 Words>

My Comment	☐ Good		
	☐ Excellent		

Parent's Comment	☐ Good	☐ Excellent
Teacher's Comment	☐ Good	☐ Excellent

🌱 Sentence Practice

A. Choose the correct words and rewrite the sentences.

Q: What do you need to make sandwiches?

You [need] **two pieces of** bread.
(some)

You [need] **two** eggs.
(some)

1. Put some (mustard / mustards) and mayonnaise on both pieces of the bread.

   Put some mustard and mayonnaise on both pieces of the bread .

2. Add some (vegetable / vegetables).

   _____ .

3. You can use two (slices of ham / hams).

   _____ .

4. Lay two (slices of cheese / slice of cheeses) on the ham.

   _____ .

5. You can also use some (lettuce / lettuces), tomato slices, and onion slices.

   _____ .

6. Put the eggs on (one piece of bread / piece of breads).

   _____ .

7. You can add some (ketchup / ketchups) on the top of the stack.

   _____ .

8. I really love to eat ham-and-cheese (sandwich / sandwiches).

   _____ .

B. Choose the correct words and rewrite the sentences.

Q: What makes your sandwiches so good?

I like to put **lots of** mustard on them.

I don't like to put **much** mayonnaise on them.

I don't like to put **many** vegetable**s** on them.

1. I made (a lot of / much) sandwiches to share with my friends.

   I made a lot of sandwiches to share with my friends   .

2. My mom didn't have (much / many) time to cook breakfast.

   _____.

3. I wanted to spread (lots of / many) butter on the bread.

   _____.

4. You ate too (many / much) sandwiches already.

   _____.

5. My dad wanted to add (a lot of / many) lettuce on the sandwich.

   _____.

6. My brother loved to put (lots of / many) ham on the sandwich.

   _____.

7. There were too (many / much) people to share my sandwiches.

   _____.

8. Put some boiled eggs on the bread, but not too (many / much) eggs.

   _____.

Revising Practice

A. Correct the underlined words. Rewrite the sentences.

1. The ingredients are <u>two piece of bread</u>, ham, cheese, mustard, and onions.

____

____.

2. You <u>can used</u> a knife to spread mayonnaise on the bread evenly.

____

____.

3. Place some vegetables and <u>cheeses</u> on the sandwich.

____

____.

4. You can cut the sandwich into <u>two triangle</u> with a knife.

____

____.

B. Expand the sentences below by adding the correct phrases from the box.

- in order to spread it evenly on the bread
- when we go on a picnic to the park or to an amusement park
- because it is so delicious and so easy to make

1. My favorite sandwich is ham-and-cheese. ➔ Add why.

My favorite sandwich is ham-and-cheese because it is so delicious and so easy to make.

2. You can use a knife to add the mustard. ➔ Add why.

____

____.

3. I love to make sandwiches for my family. ➔ Add when.

____

____.

Title: How to Make a Great Sandwich

I like to eat _____, and they are
easy to make. The ingredients are _____
_____ .
_____
_____
_____
_____
_____
_____
_____
_____
_____
_____
_____
_____
_____
_____

<More Than 150 Words>

My Comment ☐ Good
☐ Excellent

Parent's Comment ☐ Good ☐ Excellent
Teacher's Comment ☐ Good ☐ Excellent

🌱 Sentence Practice

A. Choose the correct words and rewrite the sentences.

Q: **What do you know about Mount Everest?**

Mount Everest is **the tallest** mountain.

It is about five times **taller than** Halla Mountain.

1. I am (taller / the tallest) than my younger brother.

   I am taller than my younger brother .

2. Olympus Mons is three times (taller / the tallest) than Mount Everest.

   _____ .

3. Helen can jump (higher / the highest) than Randy.

   _____ .

4. A person can jump three times (higher / the highest) on Mars than on Earth.

   _____ .

5. Hercules is (stronger / the strongest) man in Greek mythology.

   _____ .

6. Horses are (faster / the fastest) than dogs.

   _____ .

7. Brian is good at cooking. Danny is much (better / the best) than Brian.

   _____ .

8. Dolphins can jump (high / higher / the highest) of any animal in the water.

   _____ .

B. Choose the correct words and rewrite the sentences.

Q: **How does the gravity on Mars compare to the gravity on Earth?**
The gravity on Mars is not as strong as the gravity on Earth.
The gravity on Earth is stronger than the gravity on Mars.

1. People can jump (higher / as high as) on Mars.

   People can jump higher on Mars   .

2. Travel to the moon of a planet is (better / as good as) travel to the planet itself.

   _____

   _____ .

3. Watching two moons in the sky is (more exciting / as exciting as) than watching one moon.

   _____

   _____ .

4. Mars is (bigger / as big as) than Earth.

   _____ .

5. Jupiter is (the biggest / as big as) planet in our solar system.

   _____ .

6. The moons of Mars are not (beautiful / as beautiful as) the moon of Earth.

   _____ .

7. The gravity on Jupiter is (stronger / as strong as) than the gravity on Earth.

   _____ .

8. Earth is almost (smaller / as small as) Venus in our solar system.

   _____ .

 **Revising Practice**

A. Correct the underlined words. Rewrite the sentences.

1. If I could travel to another planet, I <u>would went</u> to Mars.

   _____ .

2. Mars has Olympus Mons, <u>taller</u> mountain in the solar system.

   _____ .

3. I want to be the first person <u>to climbed</u> to the top of the mountain.

   _____ .

4. I want to enjoy <u>watch</u> the two moons in the sky.

   _____ .

B. Expand the sentences below by adding the correct phrases from the box.

> • because the gravity on Mars is not as strong as the gravity on Earth
> • to enjoy watching many moons in the sky
> • in our solar system

1. If I could travel to another planet, I would go to Jupiter. ➢ Add why.

   If I could travel to another planet, I would go to Jupiter to enjoy
   watching many moons in the sky   .

2. A person can jump three times higher on Mars than on Earth. ➢ Add why.

   _____

   _____ .

3. Jupiter is the fifth planet from our sun and the largest planet. ➢ Add where.

   _____

   _____ .

My Final Draft

Title: Travel to Another Planet

If I could travel to another planet, I would go to _____,
the _____ planet from the Sun.

_____

_____

_____

_____

_____

_____

_____

_____

_____

_____

_____

_____

_____

_____

_____

_____

<More Than 150 Words>

| **My Comment** | ☐ Good | | | **Parent's Comment** | ☐ Good | ☐ Excellent |
| | ☐ Excellent | | | **Teacher's Comment** | ☐ Good | ☐ Excellent |